EDGWORTH TO CR

The Story of a Lancashire C[

by
Anita D Forth

Landy Publishing

2005

ISBN 1.872895.69.7

A catalogue record for this book is available from the British Library

This book is one of a limited edition of 1000 copies

Landy Publishing have also published:-

Blackburn in Focus by Alan Duckworth & Jim Halsall
Blackburn Tram Rides by Jim Halsall
A Blackburn Childhood in Wartime by Marjorie Clayton
Blackburn in Times Gone By compiled by Jim Halsall
A Blackburn Miscellany edited by Bob Dobson
Preston in Focus by Stephen Sartin
A Preston Mixture edited by Bob Dobson
Accrington's Changing Face by Frank Watson & Bob Dobson
Accrington's Public Transport 1886-1986 by Robert Rush
Oswaldtwistle Observed by Mike Booth & Albert Wilkinson
A full list is available from: - Landy Publishing
'Acorns'
3 Staining Rise
Staining
Blackpool
FY3 0BU
Tel/Fax 01253 895678

Designed By Anita D Forth
Printed by Nayler The Printer, Church, Accrington
Tel 01254 234247

Preface

The long history of *Edgworth Home*, which came to be known as *Crowthorn School* in 1953, the first branch of *The National Children's Home* (NCH), came to an end in July 2002 after providing 130 years of care to many hundreds of children in need. This book not only charts the long history of Edgworth Home to Crowthorn School, but offers an insight into what life was like for the children and staff during those years, through many personal recollections from the Home children who remember with great affection, how their young lives were changed by the loving care they received while living on the Lancashire Moors between Bolton and Blackburn.

I thank the former Home children and staff who passed on their personal recollections, photographs and documents. Margaret Higson for church record details, Paul Stone (artist and teacher) for illustration enhancement; The Bolton Library, NCH, The Lancashire Records Office, Preston and The University of Liverpool archives, for the use of early photographs and information, Brookes University, Oxford. The Methodist Recorder and lastly I thank my husband Ernie and dear friend Denise Agrafiotis for their help and encouragement during the writing of this book.

I dedicate this book to every child who benefited from the loving care at Edgworth, the carers and teachers who helped to shape the lives of the little ones in their care, and the Methodist mission, the true pioneers of childcare.

I especially mention a dear departed lady, Ivy French, who encouraged me to carry on with this book about The Edgworth Home, which she always considered her *"real home"*

Anita D Forth
March 2005

Suffer little children to come unto me, and forbid them not :for such is the kingdom of God St Luke Chapter18 verse16

In The Beginning

In 1869 Francis Horner, a Methodist minister from Dublin and Alfred Mager a strong Methodist who was at the time working at *'The London and Westminster Bank'* in London, placed an appeal in the *'Methodist Recorder'* on 2 April, to say that two young men were looking for subscriptions *"to purchase a lodging house in London to be used for Christian purposes."*

The Methodist Recorder,
General Christian Chronicle

TO THE EDITOR-Sir,—Many of the people of London who are honestly struggling day by day against poverty in its hardest forms, count it among their greatest hardships being compelled to live in low neighbourhoods, in company with those whose crimes they detest. But this is inevitable. Where the criminal classes effect lodgment the value of property in the vicinity decreases, and the deserving poor are drawn there by the inducements of low rents and cheap living. Such a neighbourhood is "The Mint" in Southwark. For several years a mission has been steadily carried on in the district by about twenty gentlemen, who hold suitable religious services in the kitchens of about fifteen lodging-houses every Sunday evening, visit the people at their "homes'" assist the deserving, and endeavour to carry the light and blessing of the Gospel into this truly dark region. A small mission-room has been opened in the centre of the district, which is used upon every night in the week for Bible-classes and meetings of various kinds. It is, but a cellar, but the light of heaven has found its way there, to the joy of many who before walked in "darkness which might be felt." It has long been the earnest desire of those actively engaged in the work to establish a model lodging-house in the neighbourhood, where those who are struggling to do right might have better accommodation and enjoy the incalculable benefits of a Christian home. There is fear that the house may meanwhile be sold. I ask on behalf of the commitee help in the good work from the readers of the Recorder. I will be happy to furnish further information concerning the project to those desiring it, and subscriptions will be gratefully received by yours most faithfully.

34,Lime street,EC.   FRANCIS HORNER, Hon.Sec

"To Seek and to Save that which is Lost"

The founders of the National Children's Home

Including Horner, Stephenson, Mager and Barlow

Both Horner and Mager were strong Methodists who had become increasingly concerned by the plight of the numbers of children to be found living rough on the streets of London. They felt a great need to do something for these destitute children. The two men soon received a reply to their appeal from the Revd Thomas Bowman Stephenson; the meeting of these three men was to bring about the formation of one of the most successful charitable organisations of our time, NCH-The National Children's Homes. The organisation's motto became *To seek and to save*. Stephenson was a young Methodist minister in charge of the chapel in Waterloo Road, in the East End of London. Before his appointment as minister in 1860 and his arrival in Lambeth in 1868, Stephenson's spiritual work had been in Norwich, Manchester and Bolton. This experience gave him a greater understanding of the

6

problems of the poor, the people most in need of his help. Stephenson made it very clear that his work was not just a profession; he stated that *"he who intends to lift a heavy load has to get beneath it until it rests upon his shoulders and pity must touch the heart."*

Of the disordered lives of those he was called to minister unto Stephenson wrote in his personal journal-

"The conference put me down for Lambeth. When I received the appointment my heart shrank from going. I am trying to tell myself that all must be right, but the chapel and the neighbourhood that would be under my special care are perhaps as bad as can be found out of the bottomless pit. My parish will be in the New Cut, Lambeth, and I shall have to go to chapel every Sunday morning through a street as crowded as Bolton Market Hall is crowded on Saturday nights, with people engaged in buying and selling, and I shall have to visit garrets and cellars of the dense courts of that part of London. Altogether, there is perhaps as little to invite a man as could be found in any place, but there is this one thing that does invite me-that I shall have to go seek that which is lost. There they were ragged, shoeless, filthy, their faces pinched with hunger and premature wretchedness. I began to feel my time had come. Here were my poor little brothers and sisters sold to hunger and the devil. I could not be free of their blood if I did not do something to save some of them.

"We believe we have a divine vocation"
(A Saying by Revd Stephenson)

The Church Street Home, London

The first Children's Home was set up by Revd Stephenson in Church Street, London in a small cottage not far from the Waterloo Road Methodist Chapel. The cottage comprised of little more than a large room with a loft. The first two boys, Fred and George arrived on 9 July 1869. The pamphlet below was designed to promote their work.

STATEMENT AND APPEAL
ON BEHALF OF
THE CHILDREN'S HOME
THE OBJECT OF WHICH IS
TO RESCUE CHILDREN WHO, THROUGH
THE DEATH OR VICE OR EXTREME POVERTY
OF THEIR PARENTS, ARE IN DANGER OF
FALLING INTO CRIMINAL WAYS
'Inasmuch as ye have done it unto the least of these
My brethren, ye have done it unto me'
July, 1869.

Those early pioneers encountered many problems, not least of having to turn away children from the Home because of a lack of space. They soon realised that a much bigger property was needed to house the ever-increasing numbers of children, who were in desperate need of care - children who had been orphaned, abandoned or abused and living in squalor on the streets of London. Many were found down by the riverside sleeping in empty barrels or under tarpaulin sheets.

These children were doomed to a life of crime, or worse, without help.

In 1871, when Stephenson moved to the Bonner Road Methodist Chapel in Bethnal Green, London, he noticed a sign on a derelict factory building advertising *"Workshops to let"*. Stephenson decided to hire the former Victoria Stone & Co workshop, and after cleaning up and decorating the buildings, he opened the new children's home on October 14 that year.

The Bonner Road factory became known as *"The Children's Home"* and even though the factory was a much larger property than the previous Home, it was not long before it became evident that even more space would be required to accommodate the growing numbers of unfortunate children who needed help. It is recorded that 350 such children were housed at Bonner Road in 1913. Horner said of Stephenson, "He is known as the children's friend" "How the children loved him and gathered around him" His many talents, his interests and activities, his deep sympathies, his high ideals and his wide outlook.

During a Wesleyan conference in London, Stephenson received a message from James Barlow, successful mill owner (Barlow & Jones, Prospect Street, Bolton famous for 'Osman' towels.) He lived in the village of Edgworth, Lancashire. The message was to inform the Wesleyan conference that he was proposing to buy a property in Edgworth, which included '*The Wheatsheaf Inn*' and outbuildings, a farm plus land and that he intended to present this as a gift to Revd Stephenson for the purpose of a children's home. Mr Barlow had watched with great interest all the excellent work that Stephenson had been doing in Manchester, Bolton and London, where Stephenson had made it his life's work to provide a home for the many abandoned street children.

James Barlow (pictured), a staunch Methodist and strong Temperance advocate, bought the Wheatsheaf Inn, a farm and 80 acres of surrounding land, which, along with £5000, he presented to Stephenson for a Children's Home in Edgworth. This was not just a very generous gift to a needy cause, but the opportunity for Mr Barlow to rid the village of the Wheatsheaf Inn which had earned itself a bad reputation, not only for its Sunday drinking but also for dog fighting, cock fighting and rat baiting.–Good targets for his Methodist views.

The Children's Home badge

Stephenson's Dream

Stephenson's dream was to provide a home for these forgotten children far away from the squalor and deprivation of life on the London streets with its negative influences. He wanted to find somewhere that they could be given a second chance in life, in a clean, healthy and secure environment, where they could *"breathe God's fresh air"*, be educated and grow, learning new skills which would equip them for a better future. His dream came true when on 17 April 1872 the first group of twenty four boys and four girls arrived, with the first governor, Alfred Mager, and his wife to take up residence on the bleak moorland site in Edgworth.

One can only imagine what went through their minds. What they saw was a scene of dirt and desolation with moss and

bogland stretching out before them and a dilapidated building in need of much renovation. There were no trees, no habitations only the birds, mainly grouse, snipe and plover.

Mr & Mrs Alfred Mager

The Wheatsheaf Inn had fallen into disrepair. Stephenson referred to it as *"the square, old sinister, public house"*. Their first task was to make the Wheatsheaf building habitable.

They set to work on repairing the roof, replacing doors and, windows.

11

During this time they actually had to live and work in the building, suffering all the elements of rain and biting cold winds that are associated with this part of the Lancashire moorlands, which is 1100ft above sea level. Another major task was the draining of the swamp-like bog from the surface of the land, in preparation for the building of the Home's and cultivation of the land to sustain crops which would be much needed for the Home's existence. They also had to cut up and remove large boulders (brought down from the hills during the Ice Age) using wedges and hammers. They rolled the boulders over planks of wood across the bogs before they could begin to build or cultivate the land. Mr Mager was often heard saying to the staff and children *"Why not do it ourselves"?* He would not spend a penny of the money entrusted to the home on unnecessary hired labour if he and the children could do the work themselves. He would show a boy how to handle a hoe or fix a wedge in the quarry or plane a board, but he did not stop at these details of daily work. He sought to make the children *"raise themselves up higher"* and so when a boy hammered or sawed in the carpenters shop he had before his eyes an illuminated scroll across the wall which read:-

---

**The kingliest king once lived on earth,
a carpenter in Nazareth**

Mr Mager had a liking for inspirational words being displayed on walls around the Home. Another such notice was to be found in the cobbler's workshop-

Ho! Workers of the old time, styled
The gentle craft of leather,
Young brothers of the ancient guild
Stand forth once more together.
The red brick to the mason's hand,
The brown earth to the tiller's,
The shoe in yours shall wealth command like fairy
Cinderella's.

Home lads learning the cobblers craft

The Home boys under Mager's direction remade the entire stretch of road in front of Jubilee and Howarth house. He was often heard to quote his slogan on good workmanship:-
"Right Methods-Attention to detail- Perfectness of results".

Laying drains in front of Jubilee House

How different life must have been to those young children, who were more used to the hustle and bustle of city life in London, now transported to the peaceful countryside of Edgworth with farmland and cattle, animals never seen by many of them before. These street urchins must have been made of sterner stuff than their counterparts today.

At first, the children did not take kindly to their new life in the countryside; In fact early on a group of the older boys would cause mutiny amongst the Home children during a temporary absence of the governor, whilst Mr Major was off the branch they made sticks with leather straps to twine around their wrists and openly defied the Labour Master who had been left in charge , when they heard that Major's return was imminent they ran up the hill to the quarry to hide. They fully expected to be searched out and punished, but Mr Mager left them alone. As darkness came and it started to rain, one by one, hungry and cold they returned to the wheatsheaf, only to find that the doors were locked. They wondered what fate now had in store as they begged to be let in. The ring-leaders were punished.

One of those boys Harry, who was one of the first contingent to sail to Canada, would say to Mager later *"The best thing that ever happened to us lads was the thrashing you gave us that evening"* but it was Mrs Mager who finally cured the rioters. She talked with them and prayed with them. It is said that all those boys without exception did well later on. It would take some time for the boys to acclimatise to the Lancashire moors, but gradually they grew to appreciate the beauty, the clean air and a far healthier lifestyle. To assess the value of the Home and surroundings in monetary terms today, it would be in the millions of pounds-but the true value is in the changed lives of those rescued children, who with a pick, shovel and a spade transformed the barren moorland into a Home with a fruitful farm and a thriving, self sufficient community through Christianity, whilst gaining many useful skills for later life.

The very first 'family' at The Home 1872

Although the conditions in those early years, without the benefit of clean water supplies and central heating, must have proved very difficult for the children and staff, they set about the task of building their own community with sheer determination and hard labour. It has been well documented that the young lads toiled to help build the stone chapel and houses that still stand proudly to this day.

A young Mager in the Home Chapel

The chapel was built adjacent to the *'Wheatsheaf block'* and was one of the first buildings to be erected. Stone houses would eventually surround the Wheatsheaf block; the stone used had to be quarried by the boys from a site at the top of Crowthorn Hill. They began by removing the soil and shale from the surface, baring the rock which would be lifted using wedges, crowbars and picks. The block of sand grit stone would then be wound by crane up to the surface to be cut to shape, large blocks would be wedged apart for door heads window sills while smaller blocks would be used for walling or sets for road making. Much of this work was done by the Home boys and overseen by qualified quarrymen. Mr Mager himself appears, immaculately dressed and sporting a bowler hat in many photographs, watching over his boys at work. Evidence of the quarry can still be seen today.

"Pilgrims, they laboured day and night to build their home"

A well dressed Mager supervises the lads at work in the quarry

Anyone who has visited the Edgworth site can only stand in awe of such great feats and of the sheer hard work involved in the building of the chapel and Houses that still surround the main Wheatsheaf building. Some of the buildings would accommodate more than one House group; Springfield House had four-Springfield, Broadhead, Mager and Wadhams. Jubilee and Howarth shared the large house nearest to the lower school hall on Broadhead Road.

House Building at Edgworth

The building of the reservoir

The next arduous venture would be to set about the task of building a reservoir to supply fresh clean water to the home. The reservoir is still in evidence today, to the right at the top of Crowthorn hill. All this work was completed without the benefit of machinery that would be used today. It is a testament to those early pioneers and young lads that the reservoir is still in use today, over 130 years later.

The responsibilities of the running of the farm for the first governor, who had little or no knowledge of farming, was a daunting task, with the need to provide fresh milk and food for the Edgworth Home community. By 1879 the farm would have twenty two cows, ten calves, three horses, two colts, one foal, one donkey, two sows and twenty three 8-weeks old piglets. The setting up of the cobbler's workshop and a blacksmith's provided much needed income for the Home and created employment and training for the children in useful crafts. The bakery in the basement of the Wheatsheaf building also provided income for the Home whilst feeding the

The Home Bakery

community. An inscription on the bakery wall (later used as the stores for the Home) *"Give us this day our daily bread"* remained to be seen up until the closure of the school in 2002.

THE EARLY YEARS

The early years at the Edgworth Home were said to be 'Dickensian' with a very strict set of rules, but the general feedback from Home children, is that the love and care that they experienced as young children in care there far out-shadowed any bad feelings of a strict upbringing. Most would even say that they benefited from the strong set of Christian values they lived by. While today many would frown on such a strict regime, others would argue that childcare and education have swung too far in the opposite direction.

The arrival of the Home children in Edgworth in 1872 was not welcomed by many of the villagers, who feared the consequences of having a group of delinquents living on their doorstep. Before long however, as the Home became established and the villagers witnessed the excellent work that was being done with these children, they soon became involved in the raising of funds for the Home which they realised was a most worthy cause. Along with the affluent

 Barlow family, who lived in the village in a large house named 'Greenthorne'. Many of the staff who worked at the home over the decades were indeed local people, thereby keeping the links first begun by Mr Barlow and his family.

James Barlow was born in 1821. In 1857 he built 'Greenthorne', his grand house in the village which would be used for many gatherings both of his workers, The Methodist Church and the Edgworth Children's Home.

There was always a close involvement with the Methodist church in Edgworth. For many years the children from the Home would be seen walking down Broadhead Road to the Methodist church in orderly groups every Sunday morning for worship, dressed in their Sunday best. The local Methodist minister would visit the School to give a special service or attend an assembly. This tradition remained up to the closure in 2002. The children from the Edgworth Home (known as *'Crowthorn School'* after 1948) were to integrate with village life, joining local clubs, Scout and Guide groups, and encouraged to take part in work experience placements with businesses in the area, with much success.

New Home on the Moor

This was the realisation of a dream for Dr Stephenson. Here at the Edgworth moorland site, the children would be brought up in a Christian way of life. They would be educated and learn many new skills, working on the farm and in the quarry, helping to build the chapel and the homes that would house many hundreds of children during the next 130 years. Through records not being available, it hasn't been possible to provide an exact figure.

The lads at work on the farm and building the Homes

Dr Stephenson's aims for the Home children –

1) To develop in each child a strong moral feeling.
2) To give each child a sound primary education
3) To teach each child to use his brains/hands, that they might earn themselves a living.

Three great principles lay at the foundation of the work:–

Religion-earnest and heartfelt. In an institution which serves to be a home and school to the children in residence, religion should be the controlling element of daily life.

The family system-the separating of children into family groups. In this way, the utmost personal oversight and individual care is secured, together with the largest amount of freedom and happiness to the child.

The children- should be taught not only elementary education but should be trained to skill of brain and finger and the habit of steady and systematic work.

"Give a child these three things- The fear of God, the love of home and the habit of steady industry- and you put into the hands of that child capital which, if he will but use it, will be sufficient to provide for all his needs through life".

....

Stephenson's belief was that the best influences of early life came from mothers. This is why he set up each house with a Deaconess Sister as the head of each *"family group"*.

The Sisters were trained in the role of House Mother to see to the needs of the children in their care. Many of the early sisterhood were not paid for their work, but saw this as a Christian duty. They took on a parental role in the individual house groups and are very fondly remembered for their love and dedication. They saw this work as a Christian vocation and would devote much of their lives to the good of the unfortunate orphaned or abused little souls.

These children are dear to me
Be a mother to them, and more than a mother.
Watch over them tenderly. Be just and kind.
If thy heart is not large enough to embrace them,
I will enlarge it after a pattern of my own.
If thy are froward, call upon me for help.
If thy weary, then I will be you consolation.
If thy sink beneath the burden, I will be thy reward.

A verse above Sister Margaret's desk

The first training school for the sisterhood was opened in 1890; it was named *'Mewburn House'* and was just a short distance from the Bonner Road headquarters in London.

The Sisters were trained to focus their work on:-
1. The care of children in orphanages
2. The care of the sick in hospitals
3. To work in existing churches or missions
4. To pioneer work in villages where little is being done
5. To work in missions abroad
6. To work as Providence may open the way

 In 1898 Dr Stephenson established another training school, 'Willard House' in Bethnal Green, which would be used to train the Deaconess Sisters (pictured left) for the Children's Homes. They would learn household duties, cookery, the making of children's and clothing and nursing skills.

The training course would also include Bible studies. It was Stephenson's great desire that the Children's Home and the Wesley Deaconess Order should grow side by side, united in a common aim. His fear was that the Children's Home would become a mere orphanage, and lose its character of a great saving mission. Sister Ruth Northcote, who became the first Sister in charge at Willard House, in 1898, put together what she termed:-

"Indispensable factors of essential sisterhood"

She instilled into her pupils that:-

- o *The Children's Home is a place where no gift comes amiss, and where many and varied gifts are absolutely essential. You must be able to sew and knit, darn and to make and mend.*
- o *To see when a house or child is clean and to show unwilling boys and girls how to produce cleanliness, in house and in person.*
- o *You must be able to cook a little, to trim dresses and to make hats.*
- o *To warn those who are unruly.*
- o *To comfort the feeble minded, support the weak and be patient towards all men.*

- To answer children's questions, to read aloud to them, and pray with them and for them.
- To improve their morals and grammar and their tempers.

The Houses also employed men who were referred to as 'brothers'. Their duties were to supervise and help the boys and support them during their work skills training. The young girls were set to work in the Houses to learn all the household duties e.g., Cleaning, washing, baking and ironing, for many who would go 'into service' when they left the Home. The children who were referred to the Home came from all over the UK, They had been orphaned, abandoned, in trouble with the police or deemed 'beyond control' by their parents. It was not possible to accommodate all the children and many had to be turned away or sent to the workhouses. Mr Mager had to turn away children because there was *"no room at the Inn"*

THE CHILDREN'S HOME EDGWORTH, NEAR BOLTON.

For the rescue and nurture of Orphan and neglected children of both sexes. Is a religious and industrial institution conducted upon the family system, and entirely dependent on voluntary contributions. Children are received without election, from all parts of the kingdom ; they are fed, clothed, instructed, taught to work and ultimately started upon honest careers in life.

The Institution is unsectarian in its objects and modes of operation. Present number of inmates 100. James Barlow, Esq., J.P., Treasurer ; J. R. Barlow, Esq., B.A., Hon Secretary ; A. W. Mager, Governor. In connection with the Children's Home, Bonner-road, Victoria Park, London, and Milton, Gravesend, Kent, Rev. T. B. Stephenson, B.A., Principal.

An appeal found in the Bolton Post Office Directory 1876

Some of the children on arrival at the Home were found to be fragile through lack of nourishment, or bore the scars of abuse. The Sisters would set about the task of healing the wounds and repairing the damage done to these young souls and build up a trust with them by offering love and security in a family setting, along with other children who had suffered a similar plight. For most of these children this would be their only experience of a family life.

Jack who was transferred to Edgworth from London wrote to his friends at Bonner Road," *I wear clogs and am head of the manure cart",* Jack was another of the lads who travelled to Canada with Horner in 1873. Another lad who was in the first party was Bill, an Irish lad from the Church Street days. He became a manager of a leading commercial house and one of his own children achieved great success at University in Canada.

The climate in the country

The 1870 Education Act had highlighted the needs of deprived children. William Edward Forster, MP, Education Minister at that time, and a passionate social reformer, was elected as Liberal MP for Bradford in 1861 and was chosen by Gladstone as vice president of the Committee of Council after the 1868 general election. This gave Forster the responsibility of carrying through the House of Commons the 1870 Education Bill. He was in great admiration of the work that Stephenson was doing for children. So impressed, that Stephenson was asked by Forster to become a member of the London School Board in 1873. There had been attempts to provide more Industrial schools and reformatories and the School Board were becoming more involved with the growing numbers of delinquent boys. The idea of Dr Stephenson's to provide safety and security within a Children's Home seemed to be the answer to the problems caused by these children, who, through no fault of their own, had ended up living on the streets.

The 1870 Act set up School Boards to be paid for by ratepayers to provide the elementary education previously available only in privately-funded establishments. Such schools were often known as *'National Schools.'*

Self Help

In 1873 there was a great shortage of coal throughout England. The Home could not afford to pay the high prices being asked, but since it was so dependant on coal for heating and cooking, the management had to take stock of the situation. They had the whole area surveyed, and, fortunately, a coal seam was found. A pit was sunk to a depth of 30 feet to reach the source and they had to dig out a tunnel which would provide enough space for the lads to crawl through. The coal was of such poor quality they had to supplement it with peat dug up from Crowthorn Hill, some 300 ft above the home. The work was further complicated by a water spring that continually flooded the shaft. Each day they would have to pump out the water from the shaft, before beginning work at 4 am. The children also had to dig peat from the hills above to supplement the fuel to heat the Homes.

Digging for peat on the moor

26

They loaded it onto wheelbarrows in the early years, but later used a donkey or horse and cart to transport it down Crowthorn hill. *'Old Trott'*, a cart horse on the farm became a particular favourite with the then governor, Mr Mager, although it is said that he deplored the horse's habit of chewing tobacco.

Loading the cart with peat

The Canadian Connection

In 1873 The National Children's Home and Orphanage (N,C,H,O), under Stephenson's direction began a scheme of emigration from their Homes, including Edgworth, to Canada where there was a large body of active Methodists and countless work opportunities for boys and girls, in, amongst other lines, agriculture and domestic service. The 'O' in N,C,H,O was dropped in later years when the change of emphasis moved away from orphaned or abandoned children, taking in children with learning difficulties. Edgworth Home would later close down due to this shift in emphasis, as seen in other organisations with aims similar to those of NCH.

Ready to set sail for Canada on the Polynesian, 1873

The first party of Home children, in the care of Francis Horner, one of the original founders, consisted of 49 lads and lasses. Their 10-day voyage across the Atlantic took them to Quebec then by train to Hamilton, Ontario-another two day journey. The organisation had been presented with a grand house, by a group of philanthropic Methodists and well- wishers of Ontario. The house stood two storeys high with a large veranda and balcony that spanned the whole width. There were five bedrooms. Spacious living quarters on the first and ground floors plus a washroom, scullery and ample space in the cellars. The well stocked gardens included many fruit trees and their own orchard.

The Children's Home in Hamilton

Many more such parties would follow in the years ahead. Overall, the scheme was an enormous success in improving future prospects for the emigrants. Not only were they welcomed as good labourers but many were adopted into good Christian families and their lives enriched. The total figure of those who had made that journey to Canada from the Homes in the UK was in excess of ninety thousand. It wasn't all sweetness and light even though they were a much needed work force on arrival. In years of trade depression, foreigners, even English-speaking ones were made to feel unwelcome. The Hamilton Home at 1078 Main Street East closed in 1934 after 61 years of faithful service, but new locations were found in other countries as far away as America, Australia and the Caribbean.

In a typed account by Barry Guy entitled *"Our work in Canada 1873-1934"*, he recalls the very first journey aboard the *'Polynesian'* that set sail from Liverpool in April 1873. He specially refers to two Edgworth Home lads ....

"Among the seething mass of humanity onboard was Harry, from the Edgworth branch, who had given so much trouble in the past, but he was now full of laughter and interested in every aspect of his new surroundings". Another wild, rough lad was Jack also from the branch in Lancashire. He too had been transformed there, and was now ready for a life of tree felling and ploughing in Canada."

In later years a lad from the Edgworth Home wrote of his life in Canada .... *"I was sent to a dairy farmer in London Ontario. Mr Morrison's first words when he met me were; "by golly, you're small, I doubt you'll be much use on a farm!" I was 4ft 11ins and weighed 98pounds. Having no experience I had to learn how to harness two horses allotted to me and to milk my share of 24 cows on the 150 acre farm. My lack of stature made it necessary for me to kneel on the manger to put the collars on my horses and it took some time for the puny muscles in my arms to develop a grip for milking. I had fallen in love with Canada and did not want to be sent home so I persevered until I attained some proficiency!"*

Mr Horner, recalling the train journey from Quebec, stated *"Then began the most wearisome journey over the most horrible railroad in existence, in a first class car of second rate quality! I earnestly trust that our next party may be saved the experience by our car being attached to a quicker train."*

The founders would often visit their flock in Canada. The children never forgot that they were part of Stephenson's large family and looked forward to his visits. The majority of the emigrants would go into farming, and the skills gained in

England would see others take on jobs in printing, blacksmithing and architecture. Many of the girls became servants and some were adopted into Christian families. In 1881 two Canadian universities gave honorary degrees of Doctor of Divinity (DD) to Revd Stephenson, who henceforth was referred to as Dr Stephenson.

In the archives of the Lancashire Record Office, Preston are four log books kept by successive headmasters at Edgworth. It appears that these heads were under the Governor, responsible for scholastic matters rather than for domestic and welfare. Frequently, governors such as Mr Wadhams inspected these books and signed them so as to be able to show they were keeping watch over the work of the school. For the most part, they make dreary reading but some entries give an interesting insight into school life. Teacher's absences, comings and goings are shown, along with what lectures were given by staff on diverse subjects, all called *"Object Lessons"*. The weather is often recorded, as well as the weekly half-day holiday, which wasn't always on the same day of the week.

The books cover the years 1886 to 1953 by which time the school had acquired a typewriter and become much more a part of the Lancashire County Council's Education Department. However, it is clear that from the early years of these books, the school took in *"outsiders"*, which meant children who did not live in the Home but lived in the surrounding villages.

Let's look at some of the entries in these books:-

21.10.1886 *"Mr Murphy, dentist of Bolton paid his usual quarterly visit to the school…*

25.10. 86 *"Many of the older boys away today as the potato harvest has commenced and they are required in the fields"*.
(Staff now comprising of Frederick Rydall, Head teacher, with Lucy Kay and Alice Gaskell his assistants)

············

30.4.1887 *"Report of HM Inspector received....the order is very good and all work on slates and paper is done neatly and carefully, Reading is easy and correct. Writing is good throughout...Spelling is very good except in the fourth standard. Composition is good in the sixth and seventh standards, very fair in the fifth. English and Geography are good. Arithmetic and Singing are by note are good. The few infants have been well cared for"*.

2.5.87. *"Received from Heywood's, 20 pairs of dumb-bells and 40 Callisthenic poles for use of children."* (In later years there are references to the girls giving *"wand displays"* as part of the gymnastics show)

9.6.87 *"The delegates to the conference of the Reformatory & Refuge Union being held in Liverpool this week, numbering nearly a hundred ladies and gentlemen visited the school this afternoon. The children sang three songs at their request, which by the applause, they evidently appreciated"*

June 24th to July 18th. School closed for Midsummer vacation.

30.7.87 *"There being a garden Party this afternoon and all hands required in the preparation, the children had a holiday this morning"*.

16.8.87 *"No school this morning" it being the day appointed for the annual picnic"*.

19.8.87 *"children attended funeral, of the late James Barlow Esq., the donor of the estate on which the Home is built and one who always took the liveliest interest in all that concerned its welfare. School closed in consequence"*.

....

14.8.1888 *"The Majority of boys being employed in the hay field, there was no school this afternoon"*.

27.9.88 *"As training for the scholars in "Thrift", have connected the school with the Post Office savings Bank and enrolled a number of children as depositors."*

....

5.9.1889 *"School closed this afternoon until Monday because of the preparation for the opening of the Barlow Memorial Building."*

27.9. 89 *"Mr Arthur Ankers joined the school as a head teacher."*

12.11.89 *"Dark, dismal weather made it necessary to have gas lit almost throughout the day."*

4.12.89 *"Florence Smallwood (teacher) gave a lesson on "bread making". The information was made clear by mixing the ingredients in the class"*.

....

10.8.1891 *"Total attendance, 97.....Mr John Martin commenced as head teacher,"*

31.8.91 *"No fees taken today. The managers have decided in favour of free education."*

23.9.91 *"Admitted ten new scholars that have come to live in the Institution"* (this was the first use of this word)

19.10.91. *"Admitted seven new scholars, one of whom, George A, 12 years old, can neither read nor write. He has spent but six weeks in school in his whole life".*

12.1.91 *"Mr Mager received the first instalment of fee-grant today. viz £13.17s.6d"*

... ...

12.1.1892 *"The number of scholars on the register is now about 150"*

23.1.92 *"The pupil teachers meet as usual for instruction in the morning, 7am-8am"*

1.10.92 *"Average (attendance) this week has fallen to 116. This is due to a part of the Home children having gone to Liverpool and Districts for a fortnight's singing tour. 3 or 4 boys are incapacitated owing to accidents to their hands".*

....

20.5.1893 *"A case of measles having appeared in Sanderson/Mitchell House on Thursday.... all of the children of that house, and F Smallwood, were sent home. Several outsiders were also absent from a similar cause".*

....

1.8.1894 (Staff numbers have increased – Mr Kennick, head; Martha Tomlinson, assistant; Florence Smallwood, Albert Westamacott, Roland Egerton, Lillian Teare.)

9.8.94 *"Mr Chandos Wilson of the United Kingdom Band of Hope gave a lecture to standards 4 to 7 on "Alcohol and Molecular Strength" and thoroughly interested the children."*

....

18.9.1895 *"Instead of the usual playtime I arranged, as the weather has been so hot, that the boys should have half an hour in the swimming bath."*

24.12.95 *"No School, room being decorated"*

25.12.95 *"Christmas day"*

26.12.95 *"School as usual. Miss Wade away for Christmas."*

6.1.1896 *"School, re-opened".*

....

5.2.96 *"Mr Pole, H.M.I, visited the school this morning and stayed until 12.30. This is the second visit without notice during the year….On leaving he expressed his satisfaction with the general work of the school, especially the singing."*

21.3.96 *"about 20 boys have commenced half-time work this week."*

2.11.96 *" Mr Chandos Wilson reports as follows on the papers sent up after his lecture on alcohol and the human body:- I cannot speak too highly on the excellent essay reports which the children have prepared on the lesson….They have exceeded my most sanguine expectations. To the writers and their teachers I offer my hearty congratulations."*

....

30.1.1897 *"The attendance of "outside" children has been very low this week owing to the falling snow".*

24.3.97 *"Sent J E, home this morning for a written explanation of his irregular attendance*

18.11.97 *"Louie M, lately in standard 1V in this school, died in the cottage Hospital this morning."*

27.12. 97 *"Registers marked at 1pm.Shool dismissed early, Christmas vacation commenced."*

....

22.2.1898 *"Mr Mager read and commented on Circular 413 re "Stone throwing at trains and telegraph wires."*

5.5.98 *"Admitted 20 boys, most of whom have been transferred from the Gravesend Branch of the Home".*

25.7.98 *"re-opened the school with a rather small attendance owing to the hay harvest not yet being over."*

22.10.98 *"Cicely N, a girl from our 7th standard, who will be 15 on in November, sat as "candidate" under Art 25 of the code and has been employed since in the school".*

23.11.98 *"A heavy fall of snow took place during the night. The drifts in some places were 4 or 5 feet deep. Scarcely any outside children present in consequence."*

The Edgworth Branch and its Benefactor

The family spirit of the *"Edgworth branch"* (as it was called by NCH) continued and when James Barlow died in 1887 10,000 people attended his funeral. In a chapel attached to the London Home, a brass plaque was placed in Barlow's memory. It carried the inscription *"Poor little women and little children trusted him"* Barlow had been the first to successfully introduce steam power to the weaving of counterpanes. He had been Mayor, chief magistrate of Bolton and a county magistrate. He was a political Liberal and president of the British Temperance League. He had many influential friends who would contribute financially to the Edgworth Home; the names of the house groups would reflect their involvement. Thomas Walker of Walker's Tannery was instrumental in the decision to set up a suitable memorial for Barlow following his death, in the form of a building on the Edgworth site, known as the *"Barlow Memorial Industrial Block"*. It would house a

model dairy, a knitting machine room, a series of handicraft shops and a swimming pool. One of the Houses was named after him.

An appeal to the public raised well over £2000 in a matter of a few days. The knitting room became a successful industry in the 1900's for the Home, producing garments and socks of the highest quality, which were sought after at a good price.

This would enhance the Home's income alongside the sale of milk and butter in Bolton. Mager insisted that the skimmed milk be kept for use in the Home. The butter was advertised as *"untouched by hand"* The apparatus in the dairy was mechanically belt-driven.

"The Barlow Memorial Institute,' pictured below, was the Barlow family's gift to the people of Edgworth which is within the Turton Parish and was built in 1909 as a memorial to their parents. The Institute continues to provide many activities throughout the year for the villagers and is the hub of the community.

The Barlow Memorial Institute, Edgworth, Turton 1909

The Barlow family would continue to provide funds for the annual trip to Southport for the children of the Edgworth Home, and a gift at Christmas for any child who did not receive one from relatives.

A garden party at Greenthorne

They also gave a birthday penny, provided holiday celebrations and regularly held garden parties at their home "*Greenthorne*" to raise funds for the home. The Barlow family are buried in the Edgworth Methodist churchyard where they had been regular churchgoers all their lives. The impressive family gravestone is not far from where the fifty Edgworth Home children and staff are buried.

Edgworth Home in the 1900's

In 1900, Stephenson was replaced as principal of NCH by Dr Gregory. The governor, Mr Mager, retired in September 1907 after completing the first 35 years in the life of Edgworth Home. A special service was held in the Home Chapel to say farewell to Mr & Mrs Mager and to see ten new probationary Sisters accepted into the Sisterhood.

The area of land now covered more than 200 acres and the Houses, built with the help of the Home boys, housed more than 300 children. Mager must have felt very proud indeed of all his great achievements and of those first groups of children who took on such an enormous task.

Dr Stephenson had appointed Harry Wadhams in 1900 as assistant to Mr Mager after he had proved himself as an excellent teacher at Bonner Road in London. It was a natural progression that he would take over the role as governor from Mr Mager.

Mr Wadhams would govern the branch until his retirement in 1935.

Mr Harry Wadams

The Great White Scourge

During 1912 and 1913, the Edgworth branch accommodated over 300 boys and girls. The Medical Officer at the time stated that the regular meals of plain food, plus the long hours of work in the bracing weather of the moorland countryside, were of great benefit to the children who had been brought from the overcrowded streets of London. There were "*only*" two deaths during those years. One of them was crippled and suffering from tuberculosis, another was said to '*also be a victim of the great white scourge.*'

The Medical Officer paid tribute to the sanatorium at the Harpenden branch, which took in many of the children who contracted Tuberculosis*('TB)'* and restored them to health.

They plough the fields

The Home boys farming the land

Many of the young boys from the Edgworth branch went into farming, both in this country, and abroad. Indeed, some of the boys who were working on farms in this country decided to save up the fare to Canada and emigrate to begin a new life in a new country, where their skills were much needed. Many farming skills were taught at the Home, including-crop growing, management of cattle, dairy work, construction and the repairing of farm implements.

The boys learning skills in the workshops

The industrial training scheme and the running of the Home at Edgworth were under government inspection and received regular sizeable grants to help with their work. This work was seen as most beneficial by the government at that time.

The belief in working with the child as a whole was as evident in those early years as in the later ones, although it has to be said that there was a greater emphasis on the religious side up until the mid-twentieth century.

The principals of the Home until then had been ministers who were placed in post by the Methodist Conference. Others followed Methodist ideals. The Methodist *'mission'* was to help the children to find personal faith in Christ and to inculcate a love for God's work. The generosity of the Methodist friends and followers throughout the world has stood out during my research. Many of the Children's Homes were gifted by the wealthy, concerned by the plight of homeless children.

Village residents

The work at the Edgworth branch continued to be successful and the Home was supported by the local villagers who would raise funds for the Home through many different events. There was a strong tie with the Methodist church in the village and the Home children became accepted as a part of the local village life.

The Home celebrated the Coronation of King George V in June 1911 by attending a joint service with the villagers. Following the service they had a special tea and took part in sporting events, culminating in a large celebration evening with a bonfire and fireworks on the recreation ground at the Home. Many such gatherings would follow involving the Home and the village.

The First World War

In 1914, 8,000 infantry soldiers were stationed at the Edgworth branch and there were two batteries of artillery in the grounds around the Home. How exciting this must have been for the children, the sight of all the soldiers, guns and horses.

Many of the Home children served their country in the two World Wars; Twenty four of them were on the front line in 1914. Sadly, many would make the ultimate sacrifice. One story tells of Arnold Oliver who gave his life for his friend. The rule '*up the line*' on the battlefront was that wherever possible the troops should have a hot breakfast, and one morning after Arnold had finished his breakfast he thought about his friend on guard who would be waiting for someone to take over guard duty. Arnold took over from his friend but minutes later Arnold was dead, killed instantly by a shell.

The children at Edgworth cultivated large areas of land for the production of potatoes and vegetables and the younger children looked after their own little allotments. This would prove vital in helping to feed the Home community during and after the war when there were food shortages and rationing. Following the war there were concerns regarding the expenses of running the home, as these had increased greatly due to maintenance costs. The effect of the war on the Home was that there were more children needing a home due to fathers being killed in action and in some cases the children were orphaned or sent to the Home because a mother could not cope on her own with her young family.

Here are two quotes from the Edgworth Home archive of documents now held at the Bolton Library:-

"Two little children, bright but weakened by want of care. Father fallen in battle. Mother died. Children left at workhouse after funeral".

"Father fighting (since killed). Mother drinking and living bad life, for neglecting children - two months imprisonment. When the sentence expired she abandoned a whole family of young children. The home broken up and six came to the Edgworth home."

... ...

In 1921, widespread strikes throughout the country would begin to affect the Edgworth Branch significantly. When fuel became unavailable, the resourcefulness of the staff would come to the fore. It was stated that one of the Sisters cooked a square meal by burning her old frock!

The Barlow Factor

In 1923 John Barlow died, the son of James Barlow, the initial benefactor of the Edgworth Home. Before his death John, along with his sister, *"Miss Alice"* had arranged a gift to cover the Home's annual subscription for years to come. Their brother, Sir Thomas Barlow, who had been the physician to Queen Victoria, King Edward VIII and George V, also sent £1,000 towards the renovation of the Wheatsheaf building, which, after 50 years, needed much repair. Mr Wadhams, who was governor at the time, said of John Barlow - *"A more perfect gentleman it was to me impossible to conceive".*

In 1924 the planned renovations to the main buildings and also to *'Woodville House'* and *'Bolton House'* were commenced to provide offices, a kitchen, stores, club room, and a staff dining room. Two new Houses were then built to accommodate the children. The two new houses were built behind *'Eric House'*. These were named *'Wadhams House'* and *'Springfield House.'* The two new Houses, which were dedicated to John and Alice Barlow, were built overlooking Bolton. From their elevated position, the views were spectacular. The new Houses were built on a curve from the South East to the North West to make the most of the daylight and sunshine, with the dining rooms facing south, unlike *'Jubilee House'* which had very little light with no windows on the South side and a living room that faced North.

The House group names

On Moorside Road were: - *Montgomery, Watson, Walker, Becket, Sanderson/Mitchell and Moscrop* Houses.
On Broadhead Road were: - *Barlow, Jubilee/Howarth, Springfield/Broadhead/Mager/Wadhams*. These House names came later as new houses were added.

Former House names–*Hadfield, Belmont, Bolton* used to be within the Wheatsheaf block. Eric House was demolished to make way for a branch hospital. Most of the Houses were named after the founders and benefactors of the Home as a fitting tribute.

An aerial view of the Edgworth Site 1980's

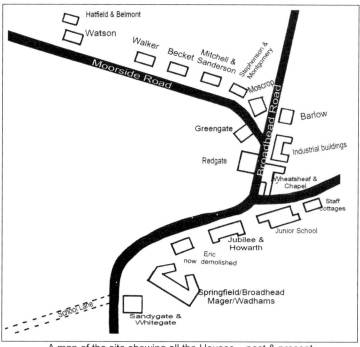

A map of the site showing all the Houses – past & present

A testimony of life

In the 1930's, a lady wrote about her time at Edgworth. In 1905, at the age of 12 yrs old, she and her sister arrived at the Home. They were orphans from the St Albans area. Her earliest memory was being given her own bed and being photographed on her second day. The photographer was the same man who made the clogs she grew to like wearing. After 3 days the two girls were placed into Stephenson/Mitchell House with 23 other girls between the ages of 3 to 16 yrs old. Rising early, prayers were said at 6.30am.Jobs followed and the girls had to learn a passage from the Bible and two verses of a hymn each week, to recite on Sunday afternoon. *"We slept in two long dormitories, each with ten beds, and a smaller room for five. Floors were bare boards, scrubbed each week."*...In the hard winters she remembered making ice cream out of fresh snow, a teaspoon of treacle and a little milk in her enamel mug. When frost was anticipated, buckets of water were thrown over the play yards to ensure there was a skating rink the following morning -*"clogs were as good as any skate"*. In their two years at Edgworth the sisters had only one visitor-their aunt from Belfast, who stayed the weekend. Visiting day was the first day of each month. Instead of hanging out stockings at Christmas, she and the rest of *"the family"* hung up their hairbrush and comb bags on the handle of the Sister's bedroom door before going to bed, *"Christmas day was the only day that the boys and girls sat down to a meal together"*

On the day of departure for Canada each year, the School assembled and sang *"Eternal Father, Strong to save"*

On leaving in 1909 she was given a tin trunk *"fitted out with three of everything"* and advice from Mrs Wadhams not to go out with members of the opposite sex without being introduced to them -*"no mention of sex at all"*.

A new Governor at Edgworth

By the time Mr Wadhams retired in 1935 he had served as governor of The Edgworth Home for 35 years, witnessed many changes and played a very large part in the Home's

success. He was remembered by the Home children as a kind and caring man. Mr Edward Shutt then became the third governor of Edgworth Home. He had trained as a teacher at Westminster College and brought with him his remarkable appreciation of literature, music and art. He was a creative man and had a great fascination for life which would influence the children in his care. He was a fine artist and had a wealth of

Mr Edward Shutt

knowledge on many subjects including astronomy, the countryside, animals, flowers & trees, bird song and ancient architecture. He loved to share his interests and knowledge with the children. He was also a very active and keen sportsman, with interests in athletics, rugby, cricket and tennis. It came as no surprise to find that under his leadership at the Edgworth branch, sport became an important part of the day-to-day life of both pupils and staff. Cups and trophies were awarded annually and competitions became the highlights of the yearly calendar. The activities for the children comprised of physical training, swimming, Cubs, Scouts, Brownies and Girl Guides. This lead to a better integration with the local communities. Under Mr Shutt's influence, the children became proficient in many sports with teams taking part in the inter-schools competitions including rounders, cricket, football, cross-country, netball and swimming.

In 1970 the school team competed against Turton Secondary School in netball and cross county winning both events, they also came first in the Swimming competition. The rounders team also played in the Bolton league and the Home's cricket team showed great promise. Considering the educational problems of these children, their outstanding achievements in the field of sport would bring much deserved praise for the Home and confidence to the children taking part.

The children would take part in many local events to raise money for the Home and their links with the wider community would prove beneficial in promoting the work of the Edgworth Home. Ted Shutt's influence on education would also see changes to the type of employment options available to the young school leavers. The girls no longer had to go into service and the boys into farming. There were now more opportunities; girls could now consider office work, shop work or nursing, some would be sent to be trained at the Highbury branch in London where a new nursery had been opened. Many boys were transferred to Harpenden branch to be trained in the printing trade.

The Second World War

In 1939, it was the 70th anniversary of the Edgworth Home and was also the centenary year of the founder's (Dr Stephenson) birthday, *"Founders Day"*, which later became the annual reunion had a much lower attendance than usual because of the impending war, which broke out on 3rd September that year. The Second World War would see a halt to the progress of building work at the Home, all the money being allocated to the building of air raid shelters and underground bunkers.

The Highbury branch in London was evacuated to the Harpenden branch and children from danger zones were relocated to safety. A group of babies and toddlers were sent to Edgworth from 'The Watson Home' in Sutton Coldfield. Edgworth prepared for war by sandbagging the basements and blacking out all the windows. The girls were relocated from John Barlow House to the Wheatsheaf block where they had fun 'camping out' in the Sister's sitting room with Sister Barbara Hill. To make up for the loss of the Sister's clubroom, the swimming baths were covered and used for 'keep fit classes' and meetings. The children would be treated to regular film and slide shows in the evenings, thanks to the gift of a new projector. One of the staff who wrote of the war years recalled the bombing of Manchester and Liverpool and of how they knew that when the phone rang at Edgworth, the enemy aircraft were on their way! The staff would take turns in manning the switchboard in 'Redgate House' (The Headmaster's house up until the school's closure). The senior boys would share the duties on fire watch. One night a bomb dropped in a field close to Watson House and at first it was thought it had hit the one of the houses, but luckily there was no damage to the Home. The newspapers were full of the story the next day, bringing many sightseers to the Home. A few of the boys made quite a profit showing the visitors around. Some of the more enterprising youngsters even sold bits of lead as souvenirs, claiming them to be "bits of the bomb"!

The wars would take their toll on the former Home children. 84 were killed in action in the Second World War and 122 were posted as "missing". A memorial organ was placed in the Edgworth branch chapel in 1950 in their memory. Revd John W.Waterhouse made his first official visit as the new NCH principal for the occasion.

Refugees at Edgworth

In 1948 children from Displaced Persons Camps in Germany and Denmark arrived at the Edgworth Branch. A story recalled by a Home child at that time describes his role in looking after a little German girl:-

"Inga came to Edgworth in 1948 and I was given the job of looking after her. She was just 4 years old. I had to make sure she was washed in the morning and had to brush her hair and plait it because it was very long. She was a good child and a quick learner. She was soon able to plait her own hair, and quickly picked up the English language. She used to call me DC. I was around 13 years old at the time". (Dennis Cooper: 1941-1949)

Some records are held in Bolton Library and in the NCH archives at Liverpool University and the Lancashire Record Office They give us an insight into daily life. Let's look at some.

In April 1941 to March 42, *"the Home was used as a public elementary school, and Lancashire County Council contributed £142.8s3d towards lighting, heating and cleaning."*
"The basements of Jubilee and Howarth had been used as air raid shelters."

....

In 1942. *"The Managers considered 25 applications for the vacant Headmaster's post caused by Mr Shutt moving to the Harpenden Branch. Mr Clifford Brooke, Headmaster of Ashbourne Methodist was appointed ....."There are now 15 boys and girls of the school attending Darwen Grammar school". Others of secondary school age attend Darwen Technical School and Bromley Cross Secondary Modern"* (Later known as Turton High School).

....

By 1943 *"the Manager's Committee were referring to the school as "Turton Edgworth Children's Home"*

....

1947, *"We have on the books 167 NCH children, and 11 others, a total of 178"* This figure would increase the following year to 184 then 187.

1947-1953 Crowthorn became a Secondary school for the Home children and the children from Turton and Edgworth. Those who passed the 11-plus would go to Darwen Grammar School or Darwen Tech. The others came to Crowthorn while work on the Bromley Cross Secondary school was completed.

....

1948 *"The Branch committee recommended to the managers a change of name to "Crowthorn School" It was felt that this change of name was "desirable".*

It was proposed that a Secondary Modern School at the Home be established, even though *"the proposed school would be substandard in buildings"* This would be known as *'Crowthorn School'* and it was agreed that transport would be provided to Hob Lane - it was felt that this was an absolute essential and that without it the scheme was impractical. A record player and loud speaker was put on order by the Local Authority for the use of the school. (An early illustration of an outside body funding something for the Home and the County Council's involvement with the NCH School).The governors were now calling themselves *"Crowthorn School."*

....

In 1949 *"the Headmaster was told the Manager's Committee had received with interest his report on the inauguration of a Parent Teacher Association. The number of scholars now varied between 150 and 158".*

"The Ministry of Education has directed that the school be managed and conducted as a secondary school." The official name would be *'Edgworth Crowthorn Secondary School'* and the County Council number would be 103.

．．．．．．．．．．

1950, *"from January, the price of school meals will be increased from 1s to 1s2d"*

．．．．．．．．．．

1951, *"The PTA granted 5s for each child going to the Festival of Britain, also towards the cost of a visit to Holme Moss and for prizes at speech day and other educational outings."* The first speech day was held in 1950. In the same year the first head boy and girl were appointed. *"Terry, the head boy was chosen for stability of character, consistency in everyday tasks and above all his reliability. Of the children on roll, 49% came from the village.*

Head reported that last year, 46 children left and *"as far as can be ascertained, no pupil has entered what is often referred to as Blind Alley employment."*

．．．．．．．．．．．

In1952, *"Mr Brooke's resignation was accepted and he was warmly thanked for his services during the ten years he had been the Headmaster and particularly during and since the reorganisation as a Secondary Modern School"*.

In September, Mr Baron followed Mr Brooke and by October there were 103 children *"on the roll"*, roughly half of them were NCH children" (This did not take into account Primary School children)

．．．．．．．．．．

January 1953 *"85 children on the roll, including 20 from the branch."*

September 1953 *"The Bromley Cross Secondary School" was now ready. Crowthorn School now became a Special Needs residential School and it remained so until closure".*

... ...

It happened in 1956

February, a television set was sent from Coomb branch *"for use in Sister Norah's house"* (Waste not want not)

Mr Barnard at Head Office told Mr Sadler(head) that the manufacturers of Odel toothpaste were offering to clear their stock at 6 shillings a dozen plus 1s10d a dozen purchase tax". Mr Sadler replied *"I would be very pleased to have one gross of these as long as it is in tubes".*

A letter from the headmaster to prospective adoptive parents stated: - *"cannot help about adopting a child of two years old. Children do not come to Edgworth until seven years old."*

Following a comment from the Home Office Medical Inspector that some members of staff were not having an annual chest X-ray, NCH wrote to all branches. Crowthorn's Head replied that recently a Mass Radiography Unit had visited and examined all staff and children. This took place at Bromley Cross School.

The branch used 255tons of coal, supplied by John Briggs of Bolton at a cost of 113/- per ton loose or 117/6 in bags.
A new *'Ideal'* boiler was ordered for Springfield at a cost of £341.

 Word from Head Office that *"our old friend Mr Harry Corbett of TV fame is planning to supply all branches who have not got a TV set with a suitable model"* (He was probably persuaded to do this by *Sooty* and *Sweep*).

Mr Sadler ordered six bedsteads for older children stipulating that they be 6'3"long, 2'6" wide and preferably cream in colour. Later that year Head office ordered fifty mattresses 6ft 3in long and 3ft wide from Wm Rhodes Ltd of Nottingham. At the same time he wrote to head office *"I have spent some considerable time this past week looking at the laundry bills. These varied between just over £1 to as much as £2.10s per week. I have worked out that, if it was possible to supply each family with a small Hoover washing machine, then these would pay for themselves …..One cannot of course install ten new laundry machines at once"* he went on to suggest that each House, each week, be credited with money until they had £20 in credit and able to pay for a machine.

Head Office asked him to look into it further, and a few days later he replied that *"the average (House) laundry bill was £31.17s 6d per week. The House whose bill was just over £1 only had nine children in residence."* He concluded his letter with *"Perhaps you will remember when a washing machine was installed at Coomb, the saving on the first year alone was considerable and more than paid for the cost of the machine"*. (Coomb was another NCH Home).

A list of Sisters at Edgworth; - 1956

Rosemary Barton
Vera Belsham
Gladys Bryan
Francess Corfield
Marjorie Darwin
Nora Gould
Margaret Bray
Jean Jaques
Sheila Mann

Marjorie Proctor
Margaret Rickardson
Irene Rowson
May Soberon
Hilda Tinker
May Valentine
Yvonne Warburton
Winifred White
Margaret Janney

THE
CHILD WELFARE CERTIFICATE
OF THE
NATIONAL CHILDREN'S HOME
AND ORPHANAGE

AWARDED ON THE SATISFACTORY COMPLETION OF
THE CHILD WELFARE COURSE OF THE
SISTERS' TRAINING SCHOOL
HIGHBURY PARK, LONDON, N.5

A group of Sisters including Sister Rosemary Barton in the 1950's

The Association of Friends

"The Association of Friends of Crowthorn School and The Red Lane Family Centre" was started in 1976. Their committee minutes are held in the Bolton library. Let's eavesdrop....

"1986 "discussed the recent refurbishment of the NCH caravan...the funds to send children on holiday....collecting wastepaper.... "1985-86 had been our most successful year financially".... The friends bought an electric clock for use in each house.... Mr Forster told of wanting to use the Sports hall as a focal point in the local community, but there was a need to install showers....the development of a language laboratory will have to await the development of the "Wheatsheaf".

"The Friends organised various fund-raising events until being disbanded in July 1993 following NCH changing the system for directing donations to a central fund. At that time, £5000 was in hand, and it was agreed to let Mr Forster spend it on a children's holiday and computer equipment".

Throughout NCH there were many local support groups under the name of the *"Association of Friends"* Their purpose was to support the work of NCH. They would assist the general committee of the Home in the discharge of responsibilities and have the opportunity to share in the work of the Home as a whole, through the Methodist Conference, for the Home's management. The Friends were the cornerstone of the development of involvement of this kind. Each appointed a member to be responsible for publicity and that person kept the Home press officer informed of the Association's activities.

The main aims of the Friends were to organise:-
- o Money raising activities
- o House to house collections
- o Form new *'League of Light'* groups
- o Branch fetes and coffee mornings
- o Sponsored events
- o Informing the public of the Home's work
- o Showing films of the work
- o The maintenance of a steady increase in the Home's voluntary income.

The Association members would pay an annual subscription of 25 pence, and a life member would pay a minimum of £5.

Edgworth Friends Association members, 1989-1990
Revd Paul Davis-(chairman)
Mrs Downie-(secretary)
Mr K Wilson-(treasurer)
Mr D Colam
Mr G Cartridge
Mr D Cooke
Mrs S Beswick
Mr C Hickey
Mr J Fielding
Mr S Forster (Head)
Mrs D Mustoe
Mrs J Ogden
Sister I Rowson
Mr M Shoreman
Sister Ingrid Hitchens

Memories are made of this

The following letter was written by John *"Dickie"* Richards in 1972 at the time of the Edgworth Centenary celebrations as a means of placing his memories on record. Sadly he died in 1999. His ashes were scattered around Moscrop House.

Moscrop House
N,C,H,O,.
Edgworth
Nr.Bolton
Lancs.
1929

Dear Somebody,

I am a ten year old boy, one of three hundred children who live in a home. There are one hundred girls and two hundred boys. Each house has twenty five girls and twenty five boys. My house is Moscrop and I would like to tell you a little about my life in the home.

This is my second year. This morning at six o'clock, as on every morning, the sound of the bell echoing around the home brought me tumbling from my bed; I was wearing a blue and white striped night shirt, frantically trying to dress and make my bed at the same time, ready for the Sister's inspection. Around me the other boys were doing the same, it could have been a scene from a Charles Dickens classic.

My eyes were half closed as I set about cleaning the cutlery, anything that did not move had to be polished or scrubbed. Silently, and with fingers crossed, I had my work inspected by Sister, talking was not allowed. I then hurried off to have a strip wash before breakfast, It would have been nice if the bacon sizzling in the frying pan had been put on my plate, instead of the Sister's. My slice of bread and treacle did not look too appetising. A cup of tea would also have tasted better than the usual mug of brown hot water, called cocoa. Dressed in corduroy, blue and white striped shirt, a stiff celluloid collar and celluloid cuffs, tie, well darned socks, and shining clogs I hurried to join the other boys to be marched to chapel by the Sister, who was dressed in her uniform of blue frock with white collar and celluloid cuffs, with a blue bonnet to match, the same blue as the police uniform. Perhaps it isn't funny looking after twenty five boys but none of the Sisters ever smile.

As the children from around the home gathered at the chapel, the sound of the iron shods on the clogs made a terrible clatter. I sat in Moscrop's allotted pew and listened to each house recite the verses of a hymn and hoped that I would remember ours. It would have been funny if every house had picked the same hymn, I thought. I am doing very well at school, although we seem to be ruled by the cane, used very much. After dinner of pea soup, I amused myself, before school, by playing cigarette cards. I lost as usual. The usual bread and treacle and cocoa for tea brings us to evening prayers and the hymn to be learnt by next Monday.

I have cleaned my clogs and the time says that another day for me is over. The days do not change, only the seasons. In the boundaries of the home, I make my own amusement.

Summer holidays are spent in the fields, haymaking, with an odd picnic at a nearby beauty spot. On fete day, I was one of the Morris dancers, I didn't see many visitors. Winter is my favourite. It is then that as a member of the concert party, I can travel all over Lancashire giving shows and meeting people. The Sister has just called me to stop writing because it is half past six, time for bed.

Goodnight.

DICKIE RICHARDS.

Home is where the heat is

The early inhabitants of the Home were to recall how cold the houses were. It would be many years before the houses would benefit from central heating.

On one of her many visits to Crowthorn School in the 1990's, Shirley Anne Field the famous actress,(born Shirley Broadbent) spoke of her time at Edgworth as a child in the 1940's, She recalled icy cold mornings in the houses that never got warm, and how the sisters would set the children to work on cleaning tasks before school. The task of scrubbing the skirting boards would help to generate some body heat, before starting the school day.

Both Shirley Anne and her brother Guy were brought up at the Edgworth Home after their mother was unable to care for them. Shirley Anne returned to the Home on many occasions to help promote the work of NCH and to visit the Home where she spent most of her childhood.

A reunion of former Home Children
Shirley Anne Field with Len Raven

A CHANGE OF NAME & EMPHASIS

The Edgworth Home changed its name officially in 1948 to *'Crowthorn School'*. No longer regarded as an orphanage, it continued to be run and funded by NCH. Many of the children would return home to their families at the weekends and during the holidays, although there would always remain a number of children who had been placed in the care of the Local Authority and needed 24 hour care. Crowthorn School would accommodate these children in their own House groups. Each House would have a group leader in charge of individual Houses along with social care staff who eventually took over the role of the Sisters. There was still one Sister at the school in the 1990's; Sister Rosemary Barton who retired in 1991. She still attends the annual reunions to meet up with

 friends and children who she used to care for.

An off-site property, *"The Red House"* (pictured left) was set up in the early 1990's at 114 Darwen Road, Bromley Cross, Bolton. This was done in an attempt to integrate the children into the local community. The children would travel to and from the School at Edgworth by bus or mini-bus from Chapeltown Road, Bromley Cross, and return home to The Red House in the evenings. The children who were placed in the Red House were all in 24 hour care. This house would never be empty; they would spend Christmas and holidays together as the *"Red House family"*.

One of the main aims of Crowthorn School in the final stage of its existence was to educate children to a standard where they could be successfully introduced back into main stream education by bringing them up to a level, educationally, with their peers. Each child would be assessed in a pre-admission review and then again on arrival at the school, when an individual programme of work would be designed both in school and the house group to suit their personal needs, educationally and socially. This would be followed by a review at six monthly intervals. Working with smaller class groups in special needs education allowed the teachers and support staff to recognise a child's strengths and weaknesses and provide whatever help was needed for that child. The child's confidence would be built up in a short time due to the provision of a 24-hour curriculum and care support system. This was to be the winning formula that led to many referrals by various Local Authorities countrywide who knew of the excellent results achieved by Crowthorn School over the years. The focus on dealing with a child as a whole, and not just his or her educational needs formed the basis of the School's ethos right up until its closure in 2002. What had begun as a structure of care in the Edgworth home, with the love and care of the Sisters and staff, would continue with the input of motivational Special Needs teachers, education professionals and support staff in the Crowthorn School day and the social care staff when the children returned to their house group. This became the foundation of the 24 hour curriculum and individual educational programmes. These formulas worked so successfully for many of the children placed there that some would return to mainstream education and to live with their own families. A few of the children referred during the 1990's would become day pupils, returning to their own homes at the end of the school day. The majority still remained in residence, only returning to their family homes during holidays and for pre-arranged weekends. As the child progressed, this would be fed back in six monthly reviews; the reviews would involve the headmaster, parents or guardians, teachers, teaching assistants, house staff, the child's social worker and an educational psychologist. The child would also be called in at some point to hear the news of his or her progress and to hear about important decisions and plans for their future. Other professionals, such as speech therapists, nurses and support workers who had been assigned to that child, would be called in where needed.

....

Friends & Family Reunited

Before closure in 2002, a reunion took place in May each year at the Edgworth Home; large numbers of the former Home children would arrive on the Friday and stay in the Houses with the children to share their many happy memories with the young ones. They would meet up with childhood friends and with other Home children from different years. There was always a great sense of comradeship on these occasions. Home children would travel with their families to attend the Reunion, some from as far a field as Canada and Australia. *"The Reunion"* became a well-established tradition and over the years many of the social care staff and educational staff would become involved in the preparations for the annual event, organising food, accommodation, parties, sporting events, games and entertainment to welcome the former Home Children.

Monday was the *"big day."* It would begin in the morning with the *'Founders' Service'* in the school chapel. There would be a mixture of management, staff, former Home children, past and present pupils and the service would be taken by the minister from Edgworth Methodist Church. Since 2002 the reunions have taken place at the Barlow Institute in Turton village. NCH has offered to fund this event until 2014.

The Order of Service would include prayers and thanks to the founders and the singing of-

"The Founders' Hymn" (set to music by P Naylor)

Men of might in days of old
Builded better than they knew.
Now their works are manifold
For their purposes were true.
Serving the increasing plan
Of the growing life of man.

Stones they quarried from the earth
Bleak and barren where they trod.
Gave them shapeliness and worth
Built a temple to their God.
Lifting hands of prayer above
Lit their altar lamps of love.

Let us praise famous men
Nobly who enriched their race
Carried heavy burdens then
Left this earth a holier place
Rest the bones beneath the sod
Radiantly they walk with God

And what cloud of witnesses
Not without us perfected
Their heroic purposes
See through years established.
Wait the end with great desire
Watch us tend the altar fire. Amen.

The chapel service would be followed by lunch in the gym or and the headmaster would give a welcome speech before announcing the various events and activities planned. The Home children could then wander around the school and visit their old House groups or take part in the sporting or special events organised for them. In the evening they would attend a party in the school hall. For many years in the 1990's these were fancy dress parties and proved to be very popular, as these photographs will testify.

The man presently responsible for bringing together the Home children each year is a *"Home child"* himself. Tom Roberts, was at Edgworth from 1942 until 1948. He spent a memorable, happy childhood there and enjoyed many reunions before taking on the responsibility of organisation, from his home in Liverpool, in conjunction with the NCH staff in Warrington, and Highbury.

Tom chats with the ex- boys and girls at Reunion   Tom with 'Dickie' Richards

A Special Day

A special ceremony was held at the Edgworth Methodist church on Sunday 14 July 2002. This was led by Rev David Hamflett who conducted a very moving service at the graveside, where all the names of the Home children and staff who had been buried in the two plots since 1875 were read out.

The NCH gravestones at the Edgworth Methodist Church were renovated in 2002, instigated by one of the ex-Crowthorn staff, (1980-2000), Jack Fielding who was a group leader for his last 15 years at Crowthorn. He had become concerned that the plots where the Home children were buried in the church yard had become neglected and forgotten. Mr Fielding contacted a local firm, J Child & Son, in 2001. They very kindly offered to donate the stone and the cost of the inscription of all 50 names on the gravestones.

The renovation was paid for by the ex boys and girls of the Edgworth Home, who still meet up at the annual reunion each year, now fittingly held in the Barlow Memorial Institute.

They rest in peace, not forgotten.

Edgworth Methodist Church Records 0f Burials- NCH graves,

John Cartwright	(9)	1875	Clarence Edmond Acklan	(10)	1906
Henry James	(11)	1883	Gertrude Chaffers	(10)	1907
Martha Makin	(13)	1885	James Henry Oldham	(13)	1910
Arthur Griffiths	(11)	1885	Margaret Davies	(14)	1912
Annie Louise Harrison	(15)	1886	Rane Belcher	(16)	1912
Alice Hendley	(9)	1887	George Harry Stone	(16)	1913
Herbert Chamber	(15)	1889	Harold Venables	(7)	1918
Frank McCabe Tart	(10)	1889	Rosina Annie Milson	(28)	1918
Robert William Beadle	(14)	1890	Frederick Allan Chandler	(9)	1921
Elizabeth Southern	(15)	1890	Dorothy Ethel Webb	(13)	1922
Mary Ann Grenville	(15)	1891	Thomas Green	(13)	1923
CharlesFrederickCaulfield	(10)	1892	John Philips Griffiths	(14)	1923
George Aspinall	(13)	1893	Ellen Westwood	(16)	1923
Robert David Williams	(17)	1894	Aubrey Hutchings	(10)	1924
Arthur Frederick Owens	(16)	1895	Jenny Shackleton	(3)	1925
Esther Thompson	(18)	1896	Jack Thompson	(15)	1925
Emma Musgrave	(13)	1897	William Rowe	(21)	1927
Alfred Votier	(14)	1898	Victor Thomas James	(10)	1930
Maria Foye	(11)	1898	James Stevenson	(15)	1933
Emma Carter	(16)	1898	William Henry Hayes	(18)	1935
Edith Elizabeth Cathall	(5)	1899	Ernest Bentham	(15)	1937
Edwin Higgin	(8)	1901	Daphne Miller	(10)	1938
Edward H Jones	(8)	1901	Hetty Jane Dye	(10)	1940
Phylis Margaret Ready	(14)	1905	Charles W McGovern 4 months		1941
Charles William Slater	(4)	1905			

The Edgworth Home views

Springfield House would be the first sight encountered on the journey up from the village past the junction at the *'White Horse'* pub. This impressive stone building would take on a different character to fit each season. In Spring and Summer the view as one approached the Home would be of a grand stately building on the right, which looked down from its elevated position over the sloping greenery of the Springfield House lawns and the farmland below with flocks of sheep and springtime lambs, In Autumn and Winter the grey mists would shroud the tops of the building and it took on a much more sinister outlook. *"More like Bleak House,"* as my son once remarked as he drove along the winding country road up to Crowthorn School, where I worked for 18 years as teaching assistant 1983-2001. The panoramic views from Springfield House are truly beautiful. On a clear day you can see for miles across the countryside towards Bolton in the distance.

Springfield House

Heavy snowfall in Edgworth 1940

The heavy snowfalls in Winter would cause problems for the staff when negotiating the snow-covered, winding roads, making their way to and from work, I remember vividly during the 1990's when the snow drifted across Broadhead Road from Plantation Road, forming a wall of snow up to 2 ft high, caused by the strong North Easterly winds off the Pennines. In true Edgworth Home/Crowthorn spirit, everyone would be involved in digging a way through the snow, so that cars could get through to take us home. The snow scenes in Winter were breathtaking in every aspect. The children loved the snow and would take great pleasure in snowballing the staff, sledging, building snowmen and igloos. Following heavy snowfalls, the 563 bus from Bolton, would give up the attempt to reach its final stop facing the School. It was a treacherous route in winter. The roads would become icy very quickly as the temperature dropped lower as you drove higher and higher from Chapeltown Road, Bromley Cross and through the Edgworth village, past the crossroads and the 'White Horse' pub then onto the winding country road that led up to the school, There were deep ditches either side, which became invisible in the snow. Many a car and bus had to be dug out.

The staff had the option of staying overnight in one of the Houses with the children, if we became snowed in. Somehow, we always managed to dig our way out!

Our long journey home through the snow.
Broadhead Road, heading for the village 1990's

Memories of Edgworth and Crowthorn

The following pages contain letters and extracts from children and staff who were at Edgworth/Crowthorn from 1918 to 2001

Ivy French : 1918-1930

"My first memory which I have kept in my mind to this day. I woke up in my cot and felt that I had come from nowhere. All of a sudden

the door opened and an angel came over to my cot and stroked my head to comfort me. That angel was Sister Edith Nesbit. From that moment on she became my 'mother' in Becket house.. My real mother had become a widow in 1917 when our father was killed in France during the War at the age of 27, the year before I was born. She was left with 6 children; unable to cope, the three youngest were sent to the Edgworth Home. I was just two years old, my sister Emily was six, brother

Emily Ivy & George *George aged ten was placed in Woodville House and was only allowed to visit us for an hour each Saturday. Here my life started, like many other children as a War Orphan. I remember going for a picnic in the Summer holidays to two beautiful woods. We christened them 'Mothers wood' and 'Fathers wood' Oh what happy hours we spent there! ....Every Sunday we walked down to the Methodist church in the village. We would walk in a lined procession down the winding country road, each House group of children dressed in their Sunday best. The girls wore straw hats with pretty ribbons on... On our way back to the home, the big girls would carry me as it was a long walk for a little one.... We had a special service in the home chapel once a year when the altar steps were enhanced with purple velvet, and across it all were placed silver three-penny bits.*

Each child would walk up to the altar and pick up a three-penny bit, curtsey, and then return to their seat. When I was old enough, to go for the first time to pick up my own coin, I was so thrilled; I remember just grabbing a handful, This brought peals of laughter from the congregation…. Mr John Barlow donated the coins, one for every child at Edgworth Branch…..We all had our own jobs to do in the Houses and mine was, each weekend, to pick up all the bits of fluff out of the porch mat. I became quite an expert at that. . If anyone was naughty- the punishment was to learn, off by heart, the longest hymn in the hymn book or darn their own socks, using cotton instead of wool, not an easy task. There was never any physical punishment. I never saw so much as a slight slap given to anyone. We must have all been naughty at some time but the Sisters were so loving and kind. What patience they had…..Mrs Haddock the Headmistress had a daughter named Lillian who was the same age as me so I was often taken to their house to play with her, as I had not started school yet. Their home was magnificent and my special treat was a bowl full of Force *(now called cornflakes) with fresh creamy milk from our own dairy cows. Mrs Haddock taught me to read, write and talk. I also remember a young boy who was the baker's son his name was Jackie Gulley. I was taken to their house to watch Mrs Gulley making treacle toffee and toffee apples for the Home children to buy when we had a penny or half-penny piece, kindly given to us by visitors…. On Visitors' Day, we used to entertain the visitors by doing the maypole dance. We got pennies and halfpennies to buy Mr Gulley's delicious toffee…..Christmas was a special time, especially the Christmas Eve carol service in the Home chapel. The Sisters would form a choir and sing "Holy Night Silent Night" They truly were the "Angels of the Lord" It was such a blessing; we were so privileged to have been put into Edgworth Home, and truthfully I have mentioned in my prayers each night a big "thank you Lord" for my years at Edgworth…….Bedtime arrived* quite early after we got home from the carol service, as we all knew that Father Christmas was on his rounds. And all down the years, to this grand old age, there is only one Father Christmas to me- his name is Mr Wadhams. He would arrive during the eve of Christmas, red cloak, white beard. He carried a huge sack full of toys and came round the dormitories to shake hands with each child, with a special cuddle for little Ivy French, until I was old enough to receive his handshake.....On Christmas Day we assembled outside the Sisters' bedrooms and sang "Christmas Awake" and two gentle voices would say "come in children"....We must have appeared like a wild mob as we rushed around their bedroom looking for our name tag on a pillow case full of toys, books and sweets..... We would all go to the main school hall for our Christmas dinner and the main treat was the huge Christmas pudding with holly and Ivy decorations on it. A sight I have truly never forgotten!....When I was 13 years of age, we were told, (completely out of the blue) that we were to go back home to our mother in Liverpool. Go Home? We **were** Home! Edgworth was the only home I had ever known. We returned broken hearted to Liverpool.

Little Ivy French with pram - 1921

May Bragg:1923-1930

"When I look back, I realise how lucky and blessed we all were to be placed at Edgworth. There were at least two hundred children at the Home. It was very strict and the boys were kept separate from the girls at all times, we had our own farm, a dairy, plenty of milk, fresh bread from our bakery, a food store, clothing store, clog shop, sewing shop, carpenters, engineers, laundry, gardens of vegetables and our own hospital with two nurses. I was in Becket House and was cared for by dedicated Sister's Nellie Read and Edna Rushton. Sister Nellie taught us to knit, sew and crochet and when she read to us, she would make the stories come alive, we would plead with her "Just one more chapter please"......We would begin the day with morning service in the chapel with the governor Mr Wadhams (a marvellous man) Christmas has never been as good as it was then. Our presents were gifts from churches and schools of Bolton, to us they were wonderful. I remember when the boys were ready to leave for Canada, we would gather outside the Home, and sang "for those in peril on the sea" How we all sobbed our hearts out. I also remember Sister Nellie taking six of us out at 4.30 in the morning clutching little bits of smoked glass, to witness Haley's comet. Something that she said we would never see again, but I did; seventy years later. It wasn't quite as exciting though the second time around.....I left the Home at the age of 15½ to go into service at a house in the village. I ended up working as a maid in a very large house in Kent. I remained there until I married in 1948....I took a very good friend up to the Home one day on one of my visits and she was so taken by it, she gave up her job and went to be trained as a Sister. She became one of the most loved and remembered Sisters at Edgworth. She is 'Sister Irene' Rowson.....I am so grateful for the happy memories which have stayed with me even though I am almost 90 years old".

Grace Baker (nee Dye): 1932-1940

"I entered the Home at the age of 4 Yrs in 1932. My younger sister Hetty was sent to Ribblesdale Home near Clitheroe. When I was 7 and my sister was 4 it was decided that sisters should be brought up together and she was transferred to Edgworth. Unfortunately Hetty died in 1940 when she was just 10 years of age and was buried in the Edgworth Methodist churchyard. I searched for Hetty's grave for many years, and in 2002, finally visited the grave after hearing about a project to restore the NCH grave…. My Mother took me away from the Home in 1940, but I have always kept in touch with Sister Evelyn Tutt (nee Salmon). She nursed my sister Hetty until she was sent to hospital where she died. Mrs Tutt is 91 years old now and still remembers her time at the home. She has been like a mother to me and a grandmother to my two daughters. I remember so much about the Home, as if it was only yesterday. The thick lumpy porridge every morning, and the cold meat on Sunday, as there was no cooking allowed on Holy day! I remember the clogs and boots we wore and the chilblains! I stuttered quite badly and I remember how Sister Nancy took time to teach me to speak properly, by the time I was 8 years old I could talk as well as all the other children….Edgworth Home was very strict and very Victorian during my time there, some of the rules and regulations would be unheard of now. We had one day out a year to Southport, most of the children were sick on the journey, because they weren't used to travelling by coach or car. There were about 210 children at the home at any one time".

Francis Barnard: 1936-1944

"My happiest memories were of the Christmas period, receiving a pillow case full of presents, watching films in the school hall. The pantomime with Mr Huddart., Easter time when we received a massive chocolate egg and Mr Huddart smashed it with a mallet before sharing it amongst the children. I also remember my duties of

taking the milk churn to the dairy to be filled in the mornings and bringing it back at lunchtime, and collecting potatoes and vegetables and getting told off by Sister Irene for feeding carrots to the donkeys! I also remember the long journey to the home from Essex".

John Kelly: 1937-1941

"I arrived at the Edgworth Branch Home in 1937 from the Newcastle branch, and on my second day was issued by Mr Etheridge, the Clogger, with a pair of clogs. They took some getting used to and my ankles were sore for a good few days. These were worn on weekdays; we had shoes for church on Sundays.....We had two labour masters at Edgworth, a Mr King and Mr Hindle. They had a building behind the school yard, and part of it was used for chopping firewood to be taken to the houses every few days by wheelbarrow. In this workshop, over the entrance door were two canes, one long thin one called 'loving kindness' and a short fat one called 'tender mercy'. So that if you had "six of the best" you could choose one or the other!......Mr Hindle was also the barber and would cut hair on Saturday mornings in the school porch; only boys of course. He had only one style- short back and sides!....We had an ancient swimming pool. In the Winter it was drained and boarded over and a billiard table installed with Mr Etheridge as our tutor. Most of the boys over 14 helped with haymaking in summer and muck spreading in winter, we usually arrived back to the Houses with as much muck on ourselves as on the fields! Another chore was stone picking in the meadows to stop the farm machinery from getting damaged.....In winter we would pile the snow against the stone walls in the fields beyond Walker House and sledge from the top field down to the road. A school friend of mine called David and I resolved to run away from Edgworth and make a home run. We boarded a train at Entwistle station and managed to get as far as Otley in Yorkshire at about midnight. As we headed out of Otley, we saw a large policeman approaching.He enquired where we were going. David, as quick as a flash, said "To visit an uncle who lives in a street nearby" The officer said "What number house does he live in?" David replied "number 28" to which the officer said "That's very strange, there are only 18 houses in that street!" We were taken into custody, given a meal, and then taken to a Young Offenders Home. The man in charge gave us some pyjamas and took our clothes away; he had a large Alsatian dog which he said would be at the bottom of the stairs in case we tried to escape. We were at this Home for three days, on the fourth day, Mr King arrived in Mr Shutt's car and we travelled back to Edgworth in style to receive six of the best for our pains!.....I left in 1941 and later joined the Grenadier Guards, where my time at Edgworth stood me in good stead".

Philip Sheppard: 1939-1941

"My happiest memories were when I had my first contact with someone I actually knew!, a Christmas card!,....when Moscrop House was top in all sports, and the day I left the Branch for good...I also remember when the Home was completely cut off by snow in the winter of 1940. Everyone had to drink an extra pint of milk and we had to start killing off some of our farm animals for food.....I was sent up to stand on Crowthorn Hill when the German invasion was expected, armed with nothing more than a two grain pitch fork!....I remember one Sunday night when Manchester was bombed just after we had assembled in the prayer hall for evening worship, and we were all sent back to our Houses. We sat up all night in the middle of Moscrop House in the connecting passage way between the dining room and the library, which was considered to be the safest place to be. When a stack of bombs fell near Belmont House, we sold pieces of guttering to the villagers as souvenirs!....I remember the army cavalry were stationed behind the Toby Inn on Broadhead Road. We found out one afternoon as they came storming down the road and I helped direct them into the field between Walker and Watson Houses. I was there for an hour or more when I should have been working on the farm…. I well remember playing football for Moscrop in my farm clogs, having no football boots! (Did anybody have any?)….Dear Sister Annie Butterworth, a true Christian worker. I can picture her now darning my socks as they always had hay seeds in them. She had the most polite manner about her, but most of all she was leading us, as I saw it... I loved her so very much and missed her presence no end after I left Edgworth…..The home was self sufficient to all respects-food, repairs etc. We enjoyed full board and lodging plus clothing and we also received pocket money- at 14 years-2d per week -15 years-3d per week and at 16 years-1 shilling per week. I left with the usual case; Bible, clothing and 19 shillings and sixpence in my bank book, I loved it at Edgworth".

Walter (Len) Raven: 1939-1950

"It is easy to focus on the negative aspects of living in a Children's Home, the youngest of 24 boys with two Sisters in charge, such as fighting or bullying, poor food and the lack of real parents and real family love and life. Somehow the years have dimmed those memories and I often wonder had Edgworth not taken me and my little sister Rita into care, what would have become of us? The authorities of the day did not want to take me (maybe because I was only 3 years old) It was only on the insistence of the then governor, Ted Shutt, who insisted he was going to keep me there. I obviously owe him a lot and remember him with great affection. In 1939, just before the outbreak of World War Two. I was placed in Becket House where I remained until September 1950. My sister went into Howarth House (aged 5), until 1948 when she went on an assisted passage to Australia with a large group of NCH children…. I remember very little about the war, apart from the deaths of the ex-Edgworth boys who were killed in some foreign place. We were so remote from it all in our little community and accepted any food shortages as normal. Besides, we had our own farm, dairy and bakery….Sports dominated my everyday life at Edgworth as we had such fantastic facilities. We had *our own football pitches, cricket grounds, swimming baths, gymnasium and athletics track, not forgetting our regular runs to the top of Crowthorn Road or up to the Toby Inn and back. Each of the Houses had their own sports team and there was rivalry to win the inter-house cup. We also competed against local teams. Academically I was never going to set the world alight! Although I was reasonable at English, Geography and Maths, I was not bright enough to go to Darwen Grammar School, which took the brighter children. The standard of education was, I think on a par with local schools. In fact, around 1948, the children from the village came up to join us…. I enjoyed the long walks across the moors with picnics. We were not above scrumping from the local orchard and were often on the mat for stealing apples. Another target (usually at night) was Mr Gulley's bakery for cakes and bread, even his well padlocked doors and windows failed to stop us! ….My memories go back to the harsh winters at Edgworth. On one occasion, the snow was so deep we were cut off (transport wise) for three weeks, another was when the governor's son was caught out on the moors during a heavy fall of snow. He sheltered in the lee of a wall and the snow drifted over and buried him. He was found 24 hours later still alive…..I remember the ingenuity that abounded when it came to making toboggans. We made the toboggans out of bits of wood and metal runners; I cannot remember where we got the materials from. They were works of art and ran exceptionally well. Our favourite run was from the top field between Walker and Watson Houses, about 100 yards down the field and over the banked up snowdrift, flying over the wall, landing on the lower field down across the lower field and out of the gate onto the road down past Watson House….. On the negative side, I remember being caught in the toilets in the playground with several other boys, being hauled up in front of the governor and the rest of the school for smoking. We were offered a choice of canes- 'loving kindness' or 'tender mercy'. I am not sure which was which or which hurt more; anyway we were given six of* the best! I only went to the toilet and didn't smoke!!....We didn't recognise bullying as such, but I remember being soundly thrashed by bigger boys on several occasions. There were no channels of redress that we dare use. However, if I learnt nothing else at Edgworth, I soon learnt how to defend myself and this has stood me in good stead....On leaving Edgworth at the age of 15 years, I went straight into The Royal Air Force, training to be an aircraft technician. In the early years I struggled, not only with the technicalities, but also to open up with my feelings regarding my background as if it was a stigma to have been brought up in an orphanage and not having proper parents. This obviously alienated me, as the other airmen went home on leave to family and friends. It took years for me to realise that others treated me for who I was and not my background........I shall always be grateful to The NCH and the Edgworth Branch for the home, love, care, education and guidance in my formative years.

Len Raven front row middle (seated) with Becket House group 1941

Dennis Cooper: 1941-1949

"I remember the choir and the concert party outings; we travelled to Manchester to a church hall in Higher Openshaw quite a few times

to perform, also to Barrow in Furness and to Lancaster. We used to stay overnight with local families....I was also in the gymnastics team and we performed at the end of every show.....Saturdays we would go to local football grounds and perform before the match, in the interval the staff would collect money from the crowds,

Dennis Cooper and his sister Barbara

those were the highlights, the discipline was very strict at the time, but it did not do us any harm".

The Edgworth Home gymnastic team

Tom Roberts : 1942-1948

"I arrived at Edgworth Home in 1942, where I remained until 1948. I will always consider myself lucky to have stayed in Moscrop House, in the same bedroom, the same bed under the same bedroom window, all the time I was at Edgworth. Looking back, I was fortunate in having the same two Sisters, Sister Hilda Tinker and Sister Jessie Bramwell looking after me. Both tried their best to give us treats during school holidays. One favourite trip of mine was up early in the morning, breakfast, make sandwiches, then walking down to Entwistle railway station, on the train to Darwen, walk to the swimming baths, have our sandwiches and Bovril at twelve o'clock, then walk down the road to the cinema to watch a film with a few sweets, before returning to the train station for our journey home.... I can honestly say that I had the time of my life at the Home. I remember the concert party and the choir visiting local church halls and chapels.... The PT display team visited the local football grounds including Bury, Rochdale, Bolton, Burnley and Blackburn, performing our display for the crowds, collecting the coppers for NCH, then being allowed to watch the match. I also recall the competitions at Edgworth. I remember, with great pride, Moscrop House winning all three cups on three occasions while I was there for swimming, cricket & football. On the last occasion I was the Captain and I was named 'Sports Boy of the Year' in'1946-47.

A winning team

83

I ache sometimes for those days gone by. I sometimes hear the laughter of friends when I visit the now silent Home....I have always tried to be involved when Reunion comes around, helping to arrange cricket and football matches for past and present pupils and staff.

In later years I helped with the arrangements for the ex boys and girls who wished to stay at the Home during the Reunion. Sister Hilda has since passed on but Sister Jessie still looks on me as one of her boys and I have spent many happy holidays with my own family at Jessie's home in Wales".

Jim Fearon: 1943-1951

"At the time I hated it at the Edgworth Home, and I showed this by constantly running away, but was always brought back to be treated again with love and affection that was selflessly given by those dedicated individuals that we knew and loved as Sisters. They were very special to all the children in their care. You didn't realise this at the time. My saddest moment came when I was transferred to the Newcastle Branch to be nearer my family home. It broke my heart and I cried my eyes out"!

Jennifer Stopforth (nee Nelson): 1945-1951

"For the most part, my time at Edgworth was happy. Having lived out in the quiet countryside before arriving at the home, it was fun mixing with other children my own age. I was given many opportunities at the Home that I would never have had. It made me the person I am today."

Sister Gladys Bryan: 1954-1976

"All my memories of Crowthorn are happy ones. I had already spent a brief time at Edgworth as a student in 1953 in Walker House, to cover for two of the Sisters, Rosemary Barton and Margaret Richardson, who attended convocation to be ordained. I arrived at

Crowthorn in 1954 after completing my training at Stephenson Hall, London. I was placed with Sister Winifred White in Broadhead, then in 1956 I was asked to go into Watson House to care for a group of boys, I remained in Watson until I left in 1976. I am still in contact with many of the staff who worked with me and boys who were in "my family" It is a great joy to meet up again at Reunions".

Sister Jean Pomeroy: 1957-1981

"For twenty five years I was a member of the House staff at Crowthorn; they were, for me twenty five years of fulfilment. The work was demanding, yet satisfying, and although at times physically tiring, there was a fellowship and friendship based on Christian principles that were comforting.

Geographically we were isolated, but the warmth and caring spirit united us in the job of caring and instruction that we had chosen to do. My recollections of the school are all happy ones.... "From my very first day at Crowthorn as a probationary Sister, I felt that this was right for me. The children were rather a mixed collection with one thing in common- the need of care, education, love and security. Crowthorn's particular standard of training and education gave the children the help they needed. I was privileged to have served as a Sister at Crowthorn. The branch will always have a special place in my memory. We did not look for miracles, but we often came close. Achieving a greater measure of stability for our young ones, who would have been without hope, if Crowthorn had not existed"

Barbara Blundell- (nee Birkenhead): 1955-1961

"I remember arriving at Crowthorn School and went to Broadhead House, where I was to stay with Sister Irene Rowson, who was the best person I ever met. She was so devoted to her job and she really cared for us all. There was never a bad day in her care.... On the day I arrived I was taken up to the bathroom to have my hair checked. Then I was taken shopping into Bolton for clothes, I really enjoyed school too, I was in the netball team and we used to go and play teams outside school, which was fun. I joined the school choir and we would sing in the church in the village on Sunday mornings, then we would sing in our own chapel in the evening.

Sister Irene Rowson

We once went to a church in Darwen to sing on "Songs of Praise." We were taken to people's houses for tea afterwards.....Occasionally, we were taken to watch Bolton Wanderers play football. These were the best days of my life..... I often tell my children about the great times I had at Crowthorn. I was so upset to hear that the school had closed. I just think of all the help and love the Sisters and staff gave to all us children. I owe them such a lot!"

Caroline Thompson-nee Riley: 1962-1966

"My happiest memories were being part of a family, feeling secure, having my first bath, being in the choir.... I remember the reunions when we used to sleep on the floor for the old girls and boys to have our beds. It was a wonderful feeling, being cared for and loved as part of a large family. I will never forget my first day at Edgworth. The children of Jubilee House were looking out of the window to see who was arriving. Sister Rosemary met me and my mum at the door. I enjoyed every minute at Crowthorn School;.... we used to dress up in old clothes and shoes from the dressing up box. I was also in the

panto at Christmas....When I arrived at Crowthorn School, I could not read a word, but when I left at the age of fifteen. I could read a whole book!"

John Stockdale : 1965-1970

"Watson House used to be girls only and the Sister in charge was a little Victorian. Apparently on wash days, if a man was seen to be approaching the House, any delicate items of clothing were hurriedly removed from the line!....Ronnie Huddart a young man at the time was sent to help move a wardrobe in Watson House. The wardrobe had to be brought down the stairs. Ronnie, being the youngest, was at the front. As they rounded the first corner at the top of the stairs, the move suddenly speeded up! Ronnie shot down the stairs, across the landing and still holding on to the wardrobe, burst open the bathroom door and fell flat on his back by the side of the bath. The Sister in charge came to see what all the screaming was about. Someone was in the bath! the Sister said loudly "Get out"! Of course he did so only after the bather and the wardrobe...My wife and I were married in 1965 and we offered to NCH our abilities. They replied that Anne was acceptable as a teacher but as a gardener I was not needed. I had to look for work off the branch. Len Scott (an ex boy from the Home) gave me a job. I later saw a job advertised at the NCH Bramhope Branch near Bradford where I came from, so I applied. Bramhope had rung to ask about me living at Crowthorn but not working there! Arthur Sadler, knowing that if I went to work at Bramhope, I would be taking a teacher (my wife) with me, suddenly found a gardener was needed at Edgworth. We lived in the School cottages. Our time at Crowthorn was blessed with a lovely daughter Elizabeth who was born in November 1968. Our lives have been enriched by some of those people that we met again at Reunion 2002. Sadly many of those I most admired have now passed on".

Sister Rosemary Barton: 1952-1991

"It is always good to hear that former pupils remember their days at Crowthorn as good times. We had no TV's, washing machines, fridges, dish washers-in fact no "mod- cons" not much money either, but we managed to have lots of fun. The work was hard but good meals, warm houses; clean beds were a treat for some of the less fortunate children.....Their progress and the response to the care made it all worthwhile for the staff....We had a lad at Crowthorn during the late fifties, early sixties. He was a good athlete and a skilful footballer and was spotted by the Manchester United scout and offered a trial. He declined because he was a Man. City supporter."

Janet Bowling (nee Purdy): 1956-1960

"My twin brother and I were seven years old when we moved to Edgworth with our parents, where my father began a teaching post. From a child's point of view we had everything; space to play, a swing park, swimming baths and lots of other children to play with. Watson House was at the bottom of our drive....One of my most vivid memories is our walk home down Moorside Road past the children's houses. The last one in the row was Walker house and after that it could get pretty scary in the winter. It was bleak and very lonely, with fields on either side. The wind whistled through the telegraph wires, which made it worse. Often by the time we reached Walker House, our friend Brian, (one of the Home children) would be waiting at his gate. We would stop for a brief chat and he would stay at his gate shouting "Cuckoo! Cuckoo!" while we walked down the dark lane, until we got within sight of the lights of Watson House, so we would not be frightened. I still remember the way he shouted Cuckoo! Summer was always an enjoyable time at Edgworth, we would picnic in the fields and build a fantastic den using sheets and a clothes horse.....I feel privileged to have lived alongside and shared the fun and games with the children at Edgworth Branch".

Jean Latham: Staff -1968-1997

"We, our family of five, arrived at Crowthorn School in April 1968 when my husband took up a teaching post. In those days all staff had to live on the premises. There were approximately 165 pupils, with the care staff, maintenance staff, farm staff, teachers and their families we made quite a large community.....Over the years I have had the privilege of meeting and working alongside some very dedicated and experienced staff, who made Crowthorn such a successful place."

Brenda Croston: 1977-1982

"I had so much love from the staff and teachers of Crowthorn School. I visited many places such as Manchester airport, Blackpool, local museums and had a memorable holiday in Carnarvon, North Wales, with my teacher Miss Shephard and all my friends from Crowthorn. It will always be "My Home". I look on all the old boys and girls as my brothers and sisters. I feel sad that other children have lost the chance to experience the love at Crowthorn, now it has closed".

Margaret Croston: 1977-1984

"I learned a lot at Crowthorn. I left school with a job waiting for me thanks to them.....I enjoyed everything about Crowthorn. Since then I have had three children and had to grow up fast. My friends are like family. That is why I look forward to reunion each year, so that I can keep up to date on what they are up to. I cannot believe that Crowthorn will not be there for future children with many different problems. There must be children crying out everywhere that Crowthorn could have helped".

Richard John Griffiths: 1995-2000

"I arrived at Crowthorn, a confused and shy child with many difficulties, but in a matter of weeks, I knew who I was and where I was going. The school taught me a great deal and got me where I am today. I lived in Howarth House and remember when brave little

Courtney died.....I made many friends at Crowthorn including my first girlfriend.....There were many laughs and good times had by pupils and staff alike.....Everyone enjoyed the trips to Grassington, where we had activities each day including swimming, horse riding and rock climbing....I looked forward to my Grandparents coming to take me to their Home in Prestatyn for weekends. I also remember being taught to ride a motorcycle and that we spent more time falling off.... It was also arranged that I attend Turton High School for some lessons and I did very well in my GCSE exams".

Anita D Forth: 1983-2001

"I will always remember my small part in the history of Edgworth Home with love and fond memories, with grateful thanks to all who made my working life so rewarding .... Headmaster's Mr Syd Rutt and Mr Stan Forster, deputy head Colin Honor, the teaching staff, care staff, office staff, the children and the ex-boys and girls who have kept in touch since closure and become good friends. I have happy memories of trips to Grassington and Dover which will stay with me forever.

I also gained many personal achievements during my time at Crowthorn and thank the excellent, motivational teaching staff for their encouragement, and all who had faith in my abilities.

During the research for this book, the long history, the facts and the Home children's stories have proved that this Home was not just any Children's Home but a very special place of safety, security and tender loving care".

The Governors and Headmasters
of Edgworth and Crowthorn

1872-1900- Alfred Mager
1900-1935- Harry W Wadhams
1935-1942- Edward Shutt
1942-1947- Clifford Brooke
1947-1956- Frederick Mulverton
1956-1975- Arthur Sadler
1975-1984- Syd Rutt
1984-2002- Stan Forster

An early photo wheatsheaf block and chapel 1800's

THE BOOK CLOSES

The stresses involved in those final years began to take its toll with a few of the most experienced staff taking early retirement. But this did not destroy the excellent support system that we as a staff had formed over many years. I felt that unique support system from the first day I arrived at Crowthorn School in August 1983 under Syd Rutt, the headmaster and Colin Honor, his deputy, then under the last headmaster, Stan Forster..... There was a great sadness felt by all who attended that last reunion to be held in the Home chapel in 2002. We had all been a part of such a great history of childcare. This wasn't just a Home; it was a caring community of dedicated people and a special home to children who would never forget the people who cared for them. For the ex-boys and girls of Edgworth Home it will always remain special to them because it was their home. Many of them had kept up the tradition of attending the annual reunion, and were very sad to see it close.

My admiration for the founders of the Edgworth Home and the work of the many dedicated staff involved through the decades in its long history inspired me to write this book so that the memories of this particular Children's Home, which became such a special home to so many, is never forgotten.

The moorland site of the Children's Home was sold to a property developer in 2003 and is set to become a residential village. The new owners are proposing to convert the 19 existing properties on the 24 acre site into a residential hamlet, including apartments, detached houses and offices. The original stone buildings are to be unchanged externally to retain the unique character of this beautiful setting. There are also plans for a permanent memorial to be placed on the Edgworth site.

A silent Crowthorn School 2003

Bibliography

Gordon Barritt - *The Edgworth Story* – (1972).

William Bradfield – *The Life of Thomas Bowman Stephenson*- (1913).

Francis Horner - *Shadow and Sun* – (1919)

John H Litten – *I Sat Where They Sat* – (1954)

Vera Rhodes Marriott- *Home on the Hill* –(195?)

Revd.H.J.Sugden – *To Seek and to Save* - (1918/19)

Barry R Guy- *Our Work In Canada*-typed account (1934) available at the Bolton Library Archives

Further Study

1) An extensive archive of documents and photographs of Edgworth Home and Crowthorn School is held in the Archives and Local Studies Section of Bolton Library: tel.01204 332185. e-mail address - archives.library@bolton.gov.uk

2) NCH archives: Sydney Jones Library, University of Liverpool Tel. 0151-794-2679

3) The Lancashire Record Office, Preston: Tel.01772 533039 www.archiveslancashire.gov.uk

4) Oxford Brookes University: The Wesley Centre, Oxford. Methodist Studies Unit: Tel. 01865 488319. www.brookes.ac.uk

Several books have been published about NCH and a few relate to the Edgworth Home. Anyone interested in further reading about Edgworth should read "*The Edgworth Story*" by Rev Gordon Barritt, who became principal of NCH in 1969.

Many of the photographs in this book are from NCH archives in the Bolton Library. My thanks are due for the use of them.

(NCH bears no responsibility for this publication)

Visit The Edgworth Home Website -
www.edgworthchildrenshome.com

The Home chapel - Reunion 2001

Tom's speech at The Barlow Memorial Institute - Reunion 2003

The ex boys and girls gather outside the Home chapel at Reunion 2001

Churches in Edgworth

The Edgworth Methodist Church
Bolton Road, Edgworth, Nr Bolton

St Anne's Church
High Street, Chapeltown,
Nr Bolton,

St James' Church
Blackburn Road
Edgworth, Nr Bolton